FRANZ LISZ

MW00785576

THE SCHUBERT
SONG TRANSCRIPTIONS
for Solo Piano

Reproduced from the 1838 Diabelli Edition

SERIES I

"Ave Maria," "Erlkönig" and
Ten Other Great Songs

DOVER PUBLICATIONS, INC.

NEW YORK

Bibliographical Note

This Dover edition, first published in 1995, is a new compilation of twelve piano transcriptions originally published separately by A[nt.] Diabelli u[nd] Comp. [Anton Diabelli & Co.], Wien [Vienna], [1838] (see individual title pages), and known collectively as *Lieder von Fr. Schubert für das Piano-Forte übertragen von Fr. Liszt*.

Features of the Dover edition are detailed in the Publisher's Note. The introduction was written specially for this edition by Dr. Rena Charnin Mueller, Department of Music, New York University.

International Standard Book Number: 0-486-28865-X

Manufactured in the United States of America
Dover Publications, Inc., 31 East 2nd Street, Mineola, N.Y. 11501

ACKNOWLEDGMENTS

For invaluable contributions to this edition, including her editorial guidance and the loan of rare Liszt publications in her private collection, we are grateful to Dr. Rena Charnin Mueller, New York University.

Thanks are due as well to the following scholars, performers and music librarians for their kind assistance in helping to prepare the present volume:

Alice Carli, Sibley Music Library, Eastman School of Music, (University of Rochester); Kendall L. Crilly and Harold Samuel, Yale University Music Library; Elizabeth Davis, Columbia University Music Library; Jane Gottlieb, Lila Acheson Wallace Library, The Juilliard School, for access to the Ruth Dana Collection of Early Liszt Editions; Leslie Howard; Fernando Laires, The American Liszt Society; Dr. Vladimir Leyetchkiss; Donald Manildi and the late Neil Ratliff, International Piano Archives, University of Maryland; Edwin A. Quist, The Arthur Friedheim Library, Peabody Institute (The Johns Hopkins University); Dr. Charles Suttoni; Dr. Alan Walker, McMaster University (Ontario); Mimi Tashiro, Stanford University Music Library; and Raymond A. White, Music Division, Library of Congress, for access to the Cedric Thorpe Davie Collection.

CONTENTS

PUBLISHER'S NOTE

Franz Liszt transcribed 55 Schubert songs for piano, including all or part of three major song cycles: the complete *Schwanengesang* (14 songs), half of *Winterreise*'s 24 settings (although all 24 songs had been announced in print), and 6 of the 20 songs in *Die schöne Müllerin* (published as *Müllerlieder*). With three exceptions,[1] the remaining transcriptions were gathered and published in three sets: *Franz Schuberts Geistliche Lieder*, *Sechs Melodien von Franz Schubert* and, as given in the full title of the present Dover volume, [12] *Lieder von Fr. Schubert für das Piano-Forte übertragen von Fr. Liszt* [Franz Schubert's Songs Transcribed for Piano by Franz Liszt].

This Dover publication reprints as a new compilation the complete *Lieder* originally published individually by Anton Diabelli and Company in Vienna in 1838. Diabelli gave the pieces consecutive plate numbers (from 6531 for "Sey mir gegrüßt" through 6542, "Ave Maria"), and all carried the common house engraving number (1133). There seems to have been no later attempt by Diabelli to issue the 12 separate pieces in a single volume.

The original music pages have been left untouched except for the editorial addition of consecutive pagination in square brackets at the bottom center of each page (for easier reference), and for general cleaning and simple restoration of details—especially staff lines and note stems—damaged by time and handling. No attempt was made to reconstruct any damaged poetic text engraved above the music. The original folios and plate numbers are retained throughout.

For easier reading, all score pages in the Dover edition have been reproduced at 125% of their original image area of 13 X 18.5 to 19 cm.

In general, information in the prefatory note to each transcription comes from two sources: for Schubert's songs, *The Schubert Thematic Catalogue* by Otto Erich Deutsch in collaboration with Donald R. Wakeling (New York: W. W. Norton, 1951; Dover corrected reprint, 1995); for Liszt's piano transcriptions, Peter Raabe's two-volume study entitled *Franz Liszt: Leben und Schaffen* (Stuttgart/Berlin: J. G. Cotta'sche Buchhandlung Nachfolger, 1931; revised edition, Tutzing: Hans Schneider, 1968).

---

[1] "Die Rose," "Lob der Tränen" and a second version of "Die Forelle" were published individually; the first version of "Die Forelle" appeared in *Sechs Melodien*. "Ungeduld" was also transcribed twice, appearing in both *Sechs Melodien* and *Müllerlieder*.

Song texts, in both German and English, are newly printed on the verso of each title page. With the exception of "Sey mir gegrüßt," newly translated for the present volume, the English translations have been drawn or adapted from three Dover publications: *Schubert's Songs to Texts by Goethe* (1979), Franz Schubert, *Fifty-Nine Favorite Songs* (1985) and *Great German Poems of the Romantic Era* (1995). Literal translations in the first and last volumes are by Stanley Appelbaum; those in the 1985 publication are by an unidentified writer.

LISZT'S SCHUBERT LIEDER TRANSCRIPTIONS

Liszt's initial foray into the transcription of music from one medium to another came in the mid-1830s with his work on the Schubert songs. Both from his artistic viewpoint and the less enlightened interests of his publishers, the venture was an immediate success. Even this early in Liszt's career, his transcriptions were, without question, extremely lucrative for his publishers, who hounded him for as many such works as he could produce. In an 1839 letter to Breitkopf, Liszt remarked that "The good Haslinger inundates me with Schubert. I have just sent him 24 new Lieder (Schwanengesang and Winterreise), and for the moment I feel somewhat fatigued with this labor."[1]

Of course, the art of transcription was not new with Liszt. What set him apart from his contemporary pianist-transcribers was his faithfulness to the original works, especially in the case of Schubert. Contrary to the given opinion, he disliked the arrangements of his virtuoso contemporaries—such as the pianist (and sometimes adversary) Kalkbrenner—because they had too many flourishes that detracted from the music, a charge that was made against Liszt as well early in his career. But Liszt ensured that his own editions would not be accused of that fault. Throughout the transcription process, he upheld the integrity of the original composer's work. In the case of the Schubert songs, Liszt took the pre-existing distinctive song accompaniments and transformed them according to his own fabulous technique. Moreover, when these song transcriptions were published, he initially objected when the original texts were printed at the beginning of each work, preferring that the words be placed appropriately throughout the score. While some publishers accommodated him (some issues of the Diabelli editions do contain underlaid texts), most found this an expensive and time-consuming procedure and printed the texts *entiers* at the beginning of each song. Liszt saw his work with Schubert in very much the same way Mendelssohn and Schumann did their work on Bach: Liszt was intent on bringing the then relatively unknown Schubert lieder into the mainstream of nineteenth-century concert repertory, as a solo performer and with fresh concert fare, alone on the stage—as Liszt put it to the Princess Cristina Belgiojoso, paraphrasing King Louis XIV, "Le concert, c'est moi!"

There is no question that Liszt took pride in the genre he helped to create, and to some extent he wished to be remembered as the composer/performer who gave the genre its unique quality. In the dedication copy of the first volume of Ramann's biography,[2] at the foot of the page containing a discussion of his transcription of the Schubert 12 *Lieder*—the works contained within this Dover volume—he added the following in the margin: "The word transcription was used by me first—similarly Reminiscences, Paraphrase, Illustration, Score for the Piano."[3] Many composers of the time were particularly delighted with Liszt's efforts, including Gaetano Donizetti and Giacomo Meyerbeer. Donizetti is reported to have written to an unnamed acquaintance: "Buy Liszt's arrangement of the March ["Marche funèbre" from *Dom Sébastien*]: it will make your hair stand on end."[4] And Meyerbeer himself wrote to Liszt in 1849, highly enthusiastic about the prospect of Liszt making a transcription from the newly premiered *Le Prophète*. Meyerbeer was not just being polite. He had first-hand knowledge of Liszt's efforts in making transcriptions accurate. He knew it was not unusual for Liszt to work from a copy of a score in order to represent the music properly, a procedure Liszt followed even as late as 1867 when he undertook a transcription from Verdi's *Don Carlo*.

Apart from his transcriptions of the Beethoven symphonies, undertaken at nearly the same time as the 12 *Lieder*, Liszt's transcriptions of the Schubert songs remain the largest such project he ever attempted. And although not finished as he had planned originally—only the 14 songs from *Schwanengesang* and 12 of the 24 from *Winterreise* were ever published—it remains unmatched as one of the most comprehensive transcription projects in the literature. Like the Beethoven symphonies, the Schubert transcriptions reproduce the original musical text reverently, with minimal flourishes and fairly strict adherence to the original strophic organization: they are among the most literal of all Liszt's transcriptions in the genre.

At the time Liszt was transcribing this music, he had written only one song of his own, a lullaby for his first daughter, Blandine, with a text by a minor poet, the Marchese Bocella, *Angiolin dal biondo crin*.[5] It is not overstating the case to say that Liszt honed his talent in writing lieder while transcribing these Schubert settings: once started in the song genre, he embarked on the composition of a remarkable series of his own songs to texts by Goethe, Heine, Hugo and Schiller. But apart from six Goethe texts that were common coin for nearly all song composers of the time,[6] Liszt never set a poem that already existed in a Schubert setting. Liszt's lieder show him to have been a quick study: he forges remarkable vocal lines with completely distinctive accompaniments, obviously inspired by the unique Schubert works.

Even in this early corpus, Liszt encapsulated many of the pianistic features that were to become the nineteenth century's stock-in-trade. Such an understanding of the color and sound of the piano was demanded by the very nature of transcribing from the song medium to the piano. The variety that the lieder genre afforded Schubert—the immediacy of a singer conveying to an audience the sense of the song by gesture, eye contact and the use of diction—all of these were unavailable to Liszt. The pianist was left the unenviable task of conveying the sense of the work by sonic means alone. Without question, Liszt's work was made easier with the advantage of new pianos by Érard and Boisselot—manufacturers who shipped their pianos all over Europe in Liszt's wake, in order to have his *imprimatur* on their latest models.[7] But in the final analysis, it is Liszt's innate feel for the resonance and voicing of the piano that motivated him with these pieces and the genre as a whole. Such considerations remain the most difficult challenges for performers to this day.

One need only look as far as the first transcription in this volume, "Sei mir gegrüßt," to see Liszt's mastery when spacing triadic sonorities. The early stanzas require tasteful balance of melody with accompaniment within one hand—a typical Lisztian technique. However, he compounds the problem in the final stanza, where he doubles the melody in octaves between the hands, contrasting each melodic line with its own widely spaced sonorous accompaniment. With the piano dynamic, and *dolcissimo teneramente* indication, the result is enthralling. Such examples of elegant registration can be found throughout the collection.

The texture of "Meeresstille" demands special mention. Although rich in harmonic overtones, the slow tempo coupled with the restrained dynamic range impose a sense of spareness on the texture, bringing to mind the immensity of a ship on a motionless sea. This almost static sound is relatively easy to transmit on today's instruments, built to sustain such long-spun sonorities. The weaker voicing possibilities of Liszt's pianos posed a monumental performance problem: producing a tone that could reach through the acoustical performance space. Here we are once again presented with Liszt's amazing ability to think ahead, to force progress, for without the barely achievable texture he wrote in 1838 the later instrument that truly realized his wanted result would not have been produced.

Commentary on Liszt's Schubert transcriptions could fill volumes, but in the present context one cannot overemphasize Liszt's mastery of large-scale tonal organization in the set. Although issued as separate items, the 12 songs are arranged in such a way that a careful and symmetrical tonal plan appears to be one of the principal factors governing the position and choice of songs in this collection. In effect, Liszt has created another Schubert song cycle out of a quite disparate group of songs, some of them very well known. In very much the same way that Liszt collected his own original and previously composed music into sets and anthologies throughout his life—for instance, the *Années de pèlerinage* and the *Harmonies poétiques et religieuses*,[8]—he fulfilled what he perceived as Schubert's promise by arranging the 12 songs so they appear to tell a story not unlike that of *Die schöne Müllerin* or *Winterreise*. From the opening "Sei mir gegrüßt" to the final "Ave Maria," the newly fashioned cycle spans another period in the life of a Schubert Wanderer: an individual in love, experiencing the seasons and natural phenomena of life, the terror of illness and death and the comfort of religion. It is a logical continuation of the well-established Schubertian thread.

On first glance, the cycle seems to revolve around the tonality of B-flat major, the keys for Nos. 1 ("Sey mir gegrüßt"), 9 ("Ständchen"—'Horch, horch! die Lerche' ['Hark, hark! The Lark']), and 12 ("Ave Maria"). However, on closer examination, the set falls neatly into three equal parts: Nos. 1–4, 5–8 and 9–12, each segment of which could be performed as an independent four-song unit or, taken together, as a complete group of 12. Each four-song group attests to Liszt's handling of types of tonal syntax that were to become the hallmarks of nineteenth-century tonal planning. Songs 1 ("Sei mir gegrüßt) and 4 ("Erlkönig") sit squarely in the key that has two flats, be it B-flat major or G minor, prefiguring the equation of relative keys that was not to become standard until after 1860. No. 2 ("Auf dem Wasser zu Singen") remains the quintessential example of the early Schubert lied that alters mode—major vs. minor—at will. The ingenuous tonal plan of No. 3, "Du bist die Ruh," stands in sharp contrast with this relatively advanced tonal thinking.

The second four-song section begins with the "Meeresstille" transcription, which, in Liszt's version, appears as a *quasi-preludio* to the three works that follow. Initially, one hears No. 5 as an extended dominant extrapolation punctuating the tonic F, the tonal center of No. 6 ("Die junge Nonne"). Then the next two songs (Nos. 7 and 8, "Frühlingsglaube" and "Gretchen am Spinnrade") complement the modal mixtures of "Die junge Nonne": Liszt carries through the F minor tonality to its relative A-flat major in No. 7 ("Frühlingsglaube"), and then extrapolates the F major sonority with that of its relative, D minor, in "Gretchen." This careful arrangement clearly shows that by the year 1838 he was able to control tonal schemes in pieces related by key signature but that shared different tonics.

Liszt initiates the final group, Nos. 9–12, with his sparkling transcription of *Horch, horch! die Lerche* in B-flat major, the same key as No. 12, "Ave Maria." These B-flat pillars again frame coupled pieces that share the same key signature but have different tonics: "Rastlose Liebe" in E major, and "Der Wanderer," initially in C-sharp minor.

Some of Liszt's publishers—notably Spina in Vienna (the successor to Diabelli), Richault in Paris and Ricordi in Milan—capitalized on his accomplishment and reissued some selections from the 12 *Lieder* in the late 1830s and early 1840s both as single numbers or in groups with alternative orderings—a process that in some cases ruined Liszt's subtle tonal organization. For this reason, Liszt's part in these subsequent reissues is questionable, although only the Richault and Ricordi editions transmit any dedication whatsoever—to the Countess Marie d'Agoult on "Ave Maria." However, all these early editions prove to be invaluable documents because Liszt's autograph sources for these works appear not to have survived.[9]

The Diabelli editions reproduced in this Dover volume all have elegant, individualized title pages that nevertheless carry similar motifs. In one way or another, the engraver included a radiant sunburst of varying dimensions, sometimes coupling it with a distinctive eight-pointed star, other times with a delicate laurel wreath. Two title pages deserve particular mention for their direct pictorial elements: No. 4, "Erlkönig," shows Goethe's fierce elf king at the top of the page, malevolently tucked behind a large sunburst; and No. 8, "Gretchen am Spinnrade," depicts Goethe's Margarete at her spinning wheel with a shadowy, faint figure hovering behind her. It is no surprise that the Goethe texts engendered the most visually compelling title pages, perhaps indicating the popularity of these two pieces in both their musical and literary incarnations.

Liszt's attention to the 12 *Lieder* did not end with their publication. These lieder transcriptions were always found on his programs, and he used them as examples in his Master Classes in his later years. It also appears that he seriously entertained thoughts of a new edition in the early 1870s, just shortly before he allowed new editions of *Winterreise* and *Schwanengesang* by Schlesinger and Haslinger: a Diabelli print of "Rastlose Liebe" was issued by Spina in 1873 for the Vienna World's Fair,[10] and this copy not only carries new engraver's markings but also extensive corrections and emendations by Liszt—clearly in preparation for a new edition. Sadly, it never materialized, and we are left to wonder at what might have been.

Unfortunately, Liszt's Schubert transcriptions never constituted part of the original Liszt *Gesamtausgabe* published by Breitkopf & Härtel from 1907 to 1936. But the popularity of these works was so great that they were among the first to be included in the Peters Edition edited by one of Liszt's favorite pupils, Emil von Sauer (1862–1942), entitled *Werke für Klavier zu zwei Händen*, begun in 1917. Sauer's dedication to Liszt's legacy cannot go unmentioned: his editions and his many recordings of the *oeuvre* are testimony to his wish to see Liszt's vision brought forward into the twentieth century.

Rena Charnin Mueller
New York, 1995

---

[1] "Le bon Haslinger d'ailleurs m'accable de Schubert. Je viens de lui envoyer encore 24 nouveaux Lieder (Schwanengesang und Winterreise), et pour le moment je me sens un peu fatigué de cette besogne." *Franz Liszts Briefe*, ed. LaMara; I (1893), p. 29.

[2] *Franz Liszt als Künstler und Mensch* (1880).

[3] "Das Wort Transcript: ward von mir zum 1ten mal gebraucht—desgleichen Reminiscences, Paraphrase, Illustration, Partition de Piano." Weimar, Goethe- und Schiller-Archiv, MS 352/1, p. 510.

[4] Walker, Alan, *Franz Liszt: The Weimar Years* (1983), p. 411.

[5] Both Lina Ramann (*Franz Liszt als Künstler und Mensch*, 1880–94) and Peter Raabe (*Franz Liszt: Leben und Schaffen*, 1931) give the date of composition for the three *Petrarch Sonnets* as c. 1839. However, the manuscript sources show clearly that these works were not written until the early- to mid-1840s.

[6] *Freudvoll und Leidvoll, Der du von dem Himmel bist, Kennst du das Land*, "Der König in Thule," *Wer nie sein Brot mit Thränen aß* and *Über allen Gipfeln ist Ruh*.

[7] See Jacques Vier, *Franz Liszt: l'artiste - le clerc* (1950), pp. 68 ff.

[8] See Mueller, "Sketches, Drafts and Revisions: Liszt at Work," in *Wissenschaftliche Arbeiten aus dem Burgenland: Die Projekte der Liszt-Forschung (1991)*, pp. 23–34; and "Liszt's Catalogues and Inventories of His Works," in *Studia Musicologica* XXXIV (1992), pp. 231–50.

[9] The only surviving fragments are sections of "Erlkönig" (including a corrected first edition with a private note to Diabelli, dated 7 August 1840), "Gretchen am Spinnrade" and an orchestral draft of "Die junge Nonne."

[10] Anton Spina had worked with Diabelli since 1824, and shortly after Diabelli's retirement in January 1851, the firm became the sole property of the Spina family.

Sey mir gegrüßt.

Lied von Fr. Schubert.

Für das Piano-Forte übertragen

von

FR. LISZT.

Eigenthum der Verleger.
Eingetragen in das Vereins-Archiv.

Nº 6531.   Pr. _ 30 x C. M.

WIEN
bei Ant. Diabelli und Comp.
Graben Nº 1133.

Paris, bei S. Richault.   Mailand, bei Ricordi.   London, bei Mori.

Sey mir gegrüßt
[GREETINGS]

Liszt's transcription: R243/1. Transcribed and published 1838.

Schubert's song: D741. Composed 1821[?]. Poem (untitled) by Friedrich Rückert. Published 1823 as Op. 20, No. 1 (No. 2 is "Frühlingsglaube," D686 [*see p. 75*]; No. 3, "Hänflings Liebeswerbung," D552).

O du Entriss'ne mir und meinem Kusse!
sei mir gegrüßt, sei mir geküßt, sei mir geküßt!
Erreichbar nur meinem Sehnsuchtsgruße,
sei mir gegrüßt, sei mir geküßt, sei mir geküßt!

O you who have been torn away from me and my kiss,
I greet you, I kiss you, I kiss you!
Accessible only to my ardent greeting,
I greet you, I kiss you, I kiss you!

Du von der Hand der Liebe diesem Herzen Gegeb'ne!
du, von dieser Brust Genomm'ne mir!
mit diesem Thränengusse
sei mir gegrüßt, sei mir geküßt, sei mir geküßt!

You who were given to my heart by the hand of love,
you who were taken away from my bosom,
with this outpouring of tears
I greet you, I kiss you, I kiss you!

Zum Trotz der Ferne, die sich, feindlich trennend,
hat zwischen mich und dich gestellt;
dem Neid der Schicksalsmächte zum Verdrusse
sei mir gegrüßt, sei mir geküßt, sei mir geküßt!

In despite of the distance, which, hostilely separating us,
has been interposed between me and you;
to the vexation of the envy of the powers of destiny,
I greet you, I kiss you, I kiss you!

Wie du mir je im schönsten Lenz der Liebe
mit Gruß und Kuß entgegen kamst,
mit meiner Seele glühendstem Ergusse
sei mir gegrüßt, sei mir geküßt, sei mir geküßt!

As you once came toward me with greetings and kisses
in the most beautiful springtime of love,
with the most fiery effusion of my soul
I greet you, I kiss you, I kiss you!

Ein Hauch der Liebe tilget Räum' und Zeiten,
ich bin bei dir, du bist bei mir,
ich halte dich in dieses Arms Umschlusse,
sei mir gegrüßt, sei mir geküßt, sei mir geküßt!

One breath of love dissolves space and time,
I am with you, you are with me,
I hold you in my arm's embrace,
I greet you, I kiss you, I kiss you!

SEY MIR GEGRÜSST.

Lied von Franz Schubert.

Für das Pianoforte übertragen

von

Franz Liszt.

D.et C. Nº **6531**.

[3]

D.et C. Nº 6531.

D. et C. N.º 6531.

6

Auf dem Wasser zu singen

(Barcarolle.)

Lied von Fr. Schubert

✳

Für das PIANO-FORTE *übertragen*

von

FR. LISZT.

Eigenthum der Verleger.

Eingetragen in das Vereins-Archiv.

N.º 6532.

WIEN

bei A. Diabelli und Comp.

Graben N.º 1133.

Pr.f 1.____ C. M.

Paris, bei S. Richault.   Mailand, bei Ricordi.   London, bei Mori.

Auf dem Wasser zu singen

[BOATING SONG]

Liszt's transcription: R243/2. Transcribed and published 1838.
Schubert's song: D774. Composed 1823. Poem by Friedrich von Stolberg, originally entitled "Lied auf dem Wasser zu singen, für meine Agnes." Published 1823; republished 1827 as Op. 72.

Mitten im Schimmer der spiegelnden Wellen
Gleitet, wie Schwäne, der wankende Kahn;
Auch, auf der Freude sanftschimmernden Wellen
Gleitet die Seele dahin wie der Kahn,
Denn von dem Himmel herab auf die Wellen
Tanzet das Abendrot rund um den Kahn.

Über den Wipfeln des westlichen Haines
Winket uns freundlich der rötliche Schein;
Unter den Zweigen des östlichen Haines
Säuselt der Kalmus im rötlichen Schein;
Freude des Himmels und Ruhe des Haines
Atmet die Seel' im errötenden Schein.

Ach, es entschwindet mit tauigem Flügel
Mir auf den wiegenden Wellen die Zeit;
Morgen entschwinde mit schimmernden Flügel
Wieder wie gestern und heute die Zeit,
Bis ich auf höherem strahlenden Flügel
Selber entschwinde der wechselnden Zeit.

Amid the glitter of the playful waves
the rocking boat glides like swans;
similarly, on the softly glittering waves of joy
the soul glides away like the boat;
for, pouring down from heaven onto the waves,
sunset dances around the boat.

Above the treetops of the western grove
the reddish glow beckons us in friendly fashion;
under the branches of the eastern grove
the sweet flag rustles in the reddish glow;
the joy of heaven and the repose of the grove
are breathed in by the soul in the reddening glow.

Ah, time escapes me
with dewy wing on the cradling waves;
let time escape again tomorrow with glittering wing
as it did yesterday and today;
until with loftier, radiant wings
I myself escape from changeable time.

AUF DEM WASSER ZU SINGEN
(Barcarole.)
Lied von Franz Schubert.
Für das Pianoforte übertragen
von Franz Liszt.

D. et C. N.º 6532.

4

Ach, auf der Freu = de sanft schim = mern = den Wel = = len

glei = tet die See = le da = hin, wie der Kahn.

Denn von dem Him = mel her =

ab auf die Wel = = len, tan = zet das A = bend=roth

und um den Kahn, tan = = = = = =

= = = = = zet das A = = bendroth rund um den

Kahn.

Ui = ber den Wi = pfeln des we = stli = chen Hai = = nes

animez peu a peu jusqu'à la fin

dimin: - - - - - -

marcato il canto

Pedale a piacere

win = ket uns freund = lich, der röth = li = che Schein.

Un = ter den Zwei = gen des öst = li = chen Hai = nes,

mf

D. et C. Nº 6532.

säu = selt der Cal = mus im röth = li = chen Schein;

un = ter den Zwei = gen des öst = li = chen Hai = nes,

säu = selt der Cal = mus im röth = li = chen Schein.

Freu = de des Him = mels und,

sempre distinto il canto

Ru = = he des Hai = = nes, ath = met die Seel" im er =

rö = thenden Schein, ath = = = = =

= = = = = met die Seel' im er = rö = thenden

Schein.

 ff appassionato

D. et C. N.º 6532.

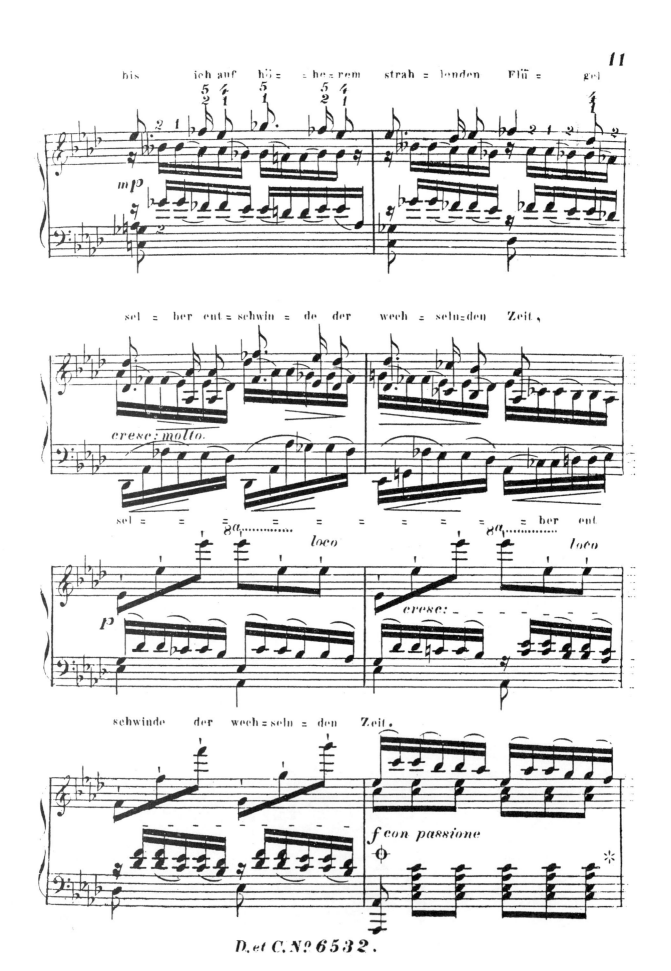

bis   ich auf   hö = he = rem   strah = lenden   Flü =   gel

sel = ber ent = schwin = de   der   wech = seln = den   Zeit,

sel = = = ber ent

schwinde   der   wech = seln = den   Zeit.

D. et C. N°. 6532

sempre più cresc: ed agitato.

D. et C. Nº 6532.

14

D.et C N.º 6532

[23]

D et C N.º 6532.

Nº 3.

DU BIST DIE RUH.

Lied von Fr. Schubert.

Für das

Piano-Forte

übertragen

von

FR. LISZT.

Eigenthum der Verleger.

Eingetragen in das Vereins-Archiv.

Nº 6533.

WIEN

bei A. Diabelli & Comp.

Graben Nº 1133.

Pr. _ 45 x C.M.

Du bist die Ruh
[YOU ARE REPOSE]

Liszt's transcription: R243/3. Transcribed and published 1838.

Schubert's song: D776. Composed 1823. Poem by Friedrich Rückert, originally untitled, later called "Kehr' ein bei mir" ["Come into My Abode"]. Published 1826 as the third of four songs, Op. 59 (No. 1 is "Du liebst mich nicht," D756; No. 2, "Daß sie hier gewesen," D775; No. 4, "Lachen und Weinen," D777).

Du bist die Ruh,	You are repose,
Der Friede mild,	gentle peace;
Die Sehnsucht, du,	you are longing
Und was sie stillt.	and that which satisfies longing.
Ich weihe dir	Full of pleasure and pain,
Voll Lust und Schmerz	I consecrate to you
Zur Wohnung hier	as a dwelling here
Mein Aug und Herz.	my eyes and heart.
Kehr ein bei mir	Come into my abode
Und schließe du	and close
Still hinter dir	the door
Die Pforte zu.	quietly behind you.
Treib andern Schmerz	Drive other sorrow
Aus dieser Brust!	out of my breast!
Voll sei dies Herz	May my heart be filled
Von deiner Lust.	with the pleasure of you.
Dies Augenzelt,	The tabernacle of my eyes,
Von deinem Glanz	illuminated by your radiance
Allein erhellt,	alone—
O füll es ganz!	oh, fill it completely.

4

DU BIST DIE RUH.

Lied von Franz Schubert.

Für das Pianoforte übertragen

von

Franz Liszt.

6

Det C. N.º 6533

[29]

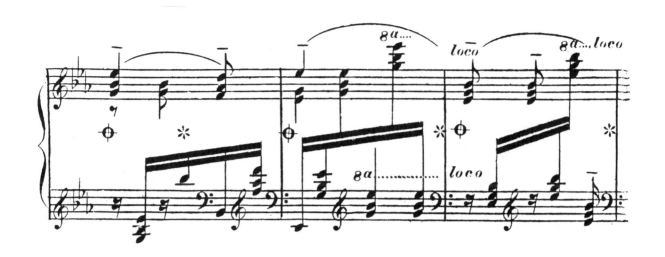

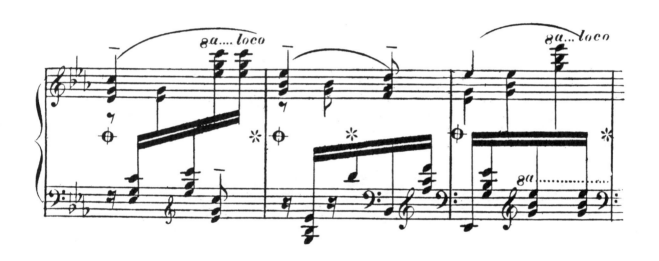

D.et C. N.º 6533.

8

8

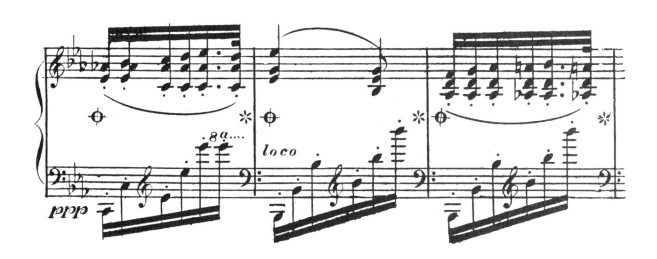

D. et C. Nº 6533.

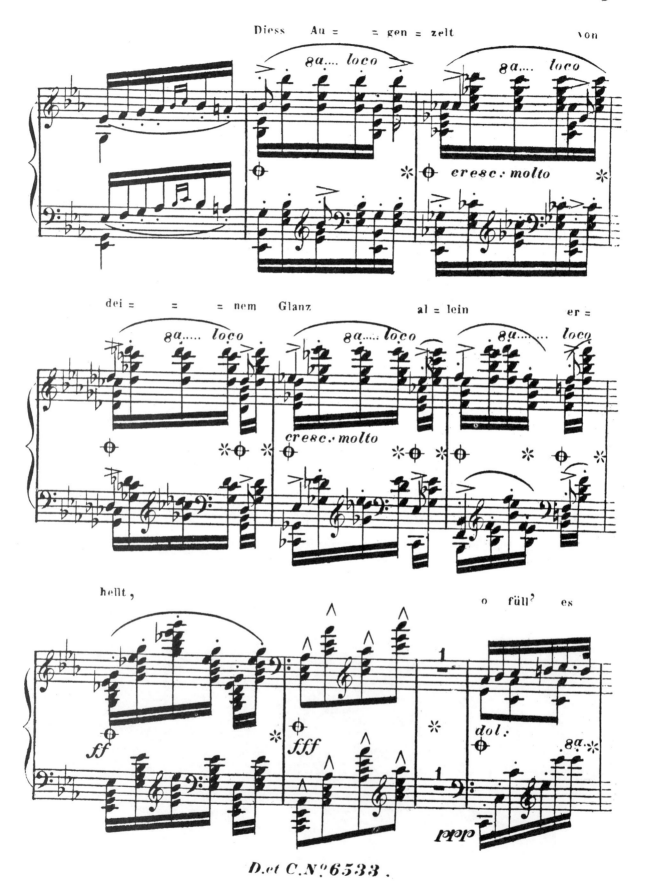

D.et C.N<u>o</u> 6533.

D. et C. Nº 6533.

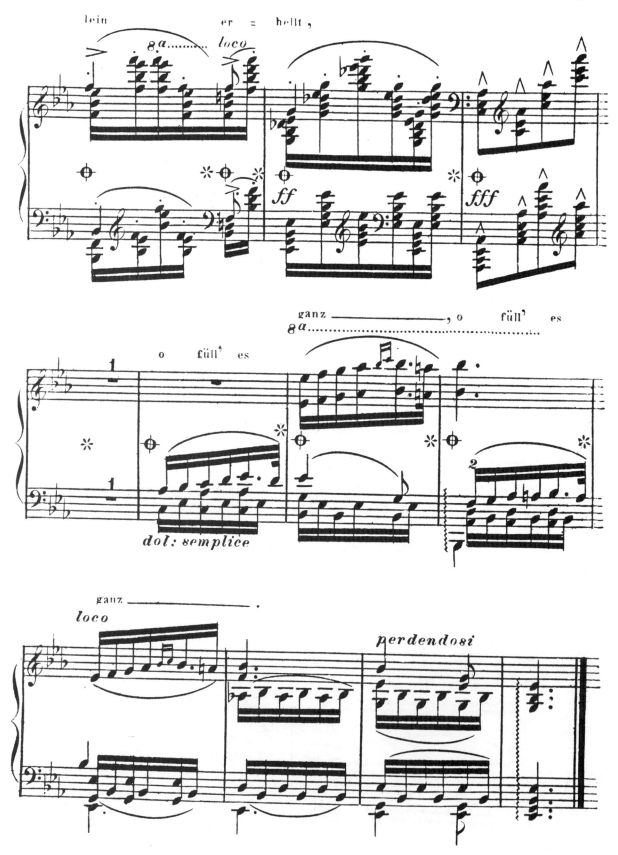

D. et C. № 6533.

ERLKÖNIG.

Lied von Fr. Schubert.

Für das

Piano-Forte

übertragen

von

FR. LISZT.

Nº 6534.

Eigenthum der Verleger.
Eingetragen in das Vereins-Archiv.

Pr. f 1.— C.M.

WIEN, bei A. DIABELLI et COMP:
k.k. Hof-u. priv. Kunst-u. Musikalienhändler,
Graben, Nº 1133.

Erlkönig

[ELF KING]

Liszt's transcription: R243/4. Transcribed and published 1838.

Schubert's song: D328. Composed 1815. Poem by Johann Wolfgang von Goethe.

Four versions of the setting, first published separately, were printed sequentially in the Complete Works Edition, Series 20, 1895. Of these, only the third version, with its lighter accompaniment, substitutes 8th notes in the right-hand part for its characteristic 8th-note triplets.

The fourth version, first published in 1821 as Op. 1—considered the definitive form of Schubert's setting—is the basis of Liszt's transcription. However, in his closing section (p. 48, *il più presto possibile*, G minor), Liszt unexpectedly introduces the "straight" 8ths of Schubert's third version, alternating measures with the triplets of the fourth.

Wer reitet so spät durch Nacht und Wind?
Es ist der Vater mit seinem Kind.
Er hat den Knaben wohl in dem Arm,
Er faßt ihn sicher, er hält ihn warm.

"Mein Sohn, was birgst du so bang dein Gesicht?"
"Siehst, Vater, du den Erlkönig nicht,
Den Erlenkönig mit Kron' und Schweif?"
"Mein Sohn, es ist ein Nebelstreif."

"Du liebes Kind, komm, geh mit mir!
Gar schöne Spiele spiel ich mit dir;
Manch bunte Blumen sind an dem Strand,
Meine Mutter hat manch gülden Gewand."

"Mein Vater, mein Vater, und hörest du nicht,
Was Erlenkönig mir leise verspricht?"
"Sei ruhig, bleibe ruhig, mein Kind;
In dürren Blättern säuselt der Wind."

"Willst, feiner Knabe, du mit mir gehn?
Meine Töchter sollen dich warten schön;
Meine Töchter führen den nächtlichen Reihn
Und wiegen und tanzen und singen dich ein."

"Mein Vater, mein Vater, und siehst du nicht dort
Erlkönigs Töchter am düstern Ort?"
"Mein Sohn, mein Sohn, ich seh es genau,
Es scheinen die alten Weiden so grau."

"Ich liebe dich, mich reizt deine schöne Gestalt;
Und bist du nicht willig, so brauch ich Gewalt."
"Mein Vater, mein Vater, jetzt faßt er mich an!
Erlkönig hat mir ein Leids getan!"

Dem Vater grauset's, er reitet geschwind,
Er hält in Armen das ächzende Kind,
Erreicht den Hof mit Mühe und Not—
In seinen Armen das Kind war tot.

Who is riding so late through night and wind?
It is the father with his child.
He has the boy firmly in his arms,
He grasps him securely, he keeps him warm.

"My son, why are you hiding your face in such terror?"
"Father, don't you see the elf king?
The elf king with his crown and train?"
"My son, it is a patch of fog."

"You dear child, come along with me!
I will play really beautiful games with you;
Many colorful flowers grow by the banks,
My mother has many a golden garment."

"My father, my father, and don't you hear
What the elf king is quietly promising me?"
"Be calm, stay calm, my child:
The wind is whistling in the dry leaves."

"My fine boy, do you want to come with me?
My daughters shall attend you beautifully;
My daughters lead the round dance at night,
And will rock and dance and sing you to sleep."

"My father, my father, and don't you see there
The elf king's daughters in that gloomy place?"
"My son, my son, I see it clearly:
The old willows have that gray appearance."

"I love you, your beautiful form arouses me;
And if you are not willing, I will use force."
"My father, my father, now he is seizing me!
The elf king has hurt me!"

The father is frightened, he rides swiftly,
He holds in his arms the groaning child;
He reaches his yard with effort and distress—
In his arms the child was dead.

ERLKÖNIG.

Lied von Franz Schubert.

Für das Pianoforte übertragen

von Franz Liszt.

D.et C.N.º6534.

4

spät   durch Nacht und   Wind?

Es   ist   der Va = ter mit

sei = = = nem Kind;   er hat den

poco rinforz:

Kna = = ben   wohl in dem Arm,   er

poco rf

D. et C. Nº 6534.

[38]

du den Erl = = = kö = nig

nicht?

mf

p

Er = = = = len = kö = nig mit

mf

Kron' und Schweif? (Der Vater) Mein

pp

D. et C. Nº 6534.

(Der Vater)

Sei

lei = = se verspricht?—

dim:

ruhig, bleibe ruhig, mein Kind; in dürren Blättern säuselt der Wind.

tranquillo.

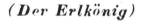

(Der Erlkönig)

"Willst fei = ner Kna = be, du mit mir geh'n? meine

PP un peu plus animé
legg: amorosamente

Töch = ter sol = len dich war = ten schön, mei = ne

D. et C. N.º 6534.

[43]

12

äch = = zen = = de Kind,

er = reicht den

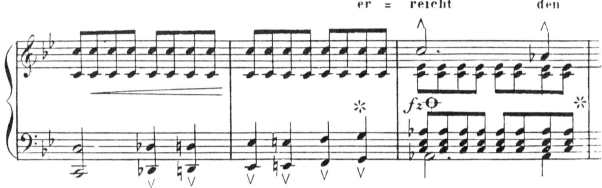

Hof mit Müh' und Noth;

in seinen Armen das Kind war todt.

Andante.

D. et C. N.º 6534.

Nᵒ 5

Meeresstille,

Lied von Fr.Schubert.

für das

PIANO-FORTE

übertragen

von

FR. LISZT.

Eigenthum der Verleger.

Eingetragen in das Vereins Archiv.

Nᵒ 6535. WIEN, Pr._30 x C.M.

bei Ant. Diabelli u. Comp.

Graben Nᵒ 1133.

Meeresstille

[CALM AT SEA]

Liszt's transcription: R243/5. Transcribed and published 1838.

Schubert's song: D216. Composed 1815. Poem by Johann Wolfgang von Goethe. Published 1821 as the second of four Goethe settings, Op. 3 (No. 1 is "Schäfer's Klagelied," D121; No. 3, "Heidenröslein," D257; No. 4, "Jägers Abendlied," D368).

Tiefe Stille herrscht im Wasser,
ohne Regung ruht das Meer.
und bekümmert sieht der Schiffer
glatte Fläche rings umher.

Keine Luft von keiner Seite!
Todesstille fürchterlich!
In der ungeheuern Weite
reget keine Welle sich.

Deep silence reigns upon the waters,
the sea is at rest without the slightest motion,
and with a worried mind the boatman
sees a smooth surface all about him.

No breeze from any quarter!
A fearful, deathlike silence!
In the enormous expanse
no wave stirs.

MEERESSTILLE.

Lied von Franz Schubert.

Für das Pianoforte übertragen

von

Franz Liszt.

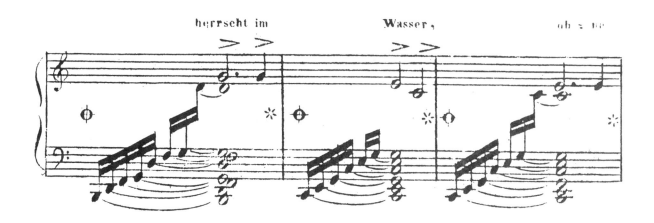

D. et C. No. 6535.

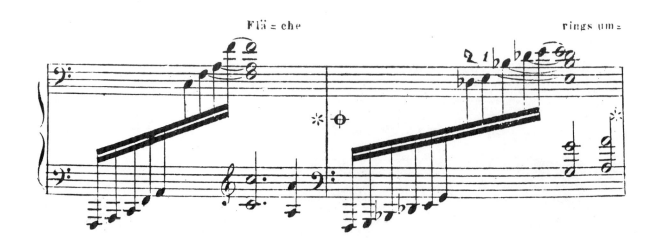

D. et C. Nᵒ 6535.

4

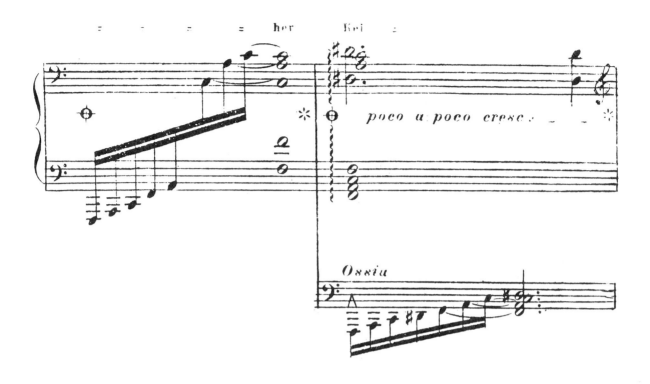

her Kei

poco a poco cresc.

Ossia

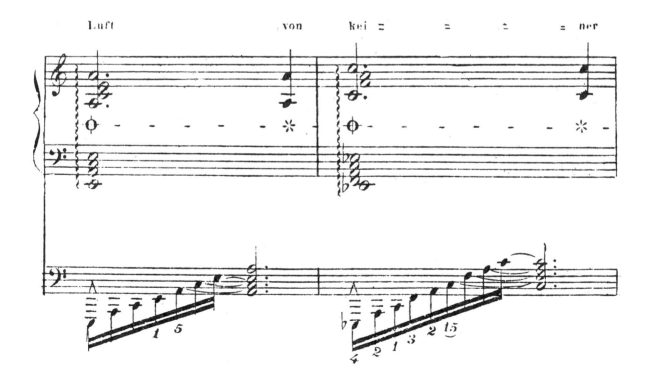

Luft   von   kei = = = ner

D. et C. Nº 6535

6

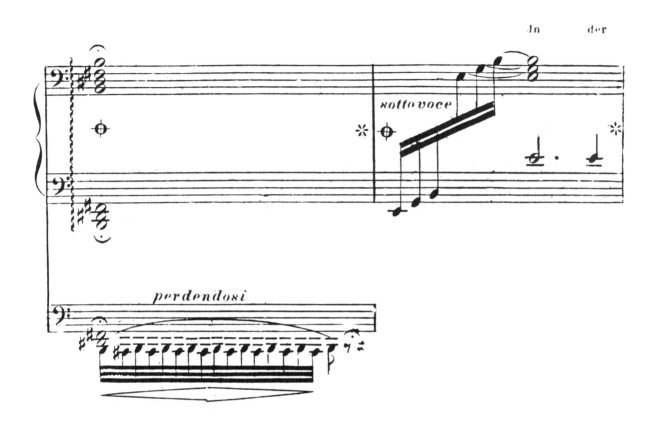

In   der

sotto voce

perdendosi

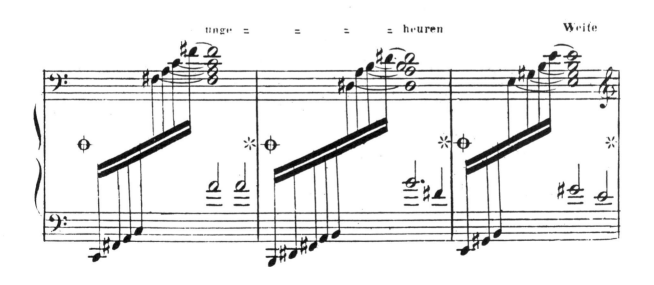

unge =   =   =   = heuren   Weite

D. et C. N⁰ 6535.

[57]

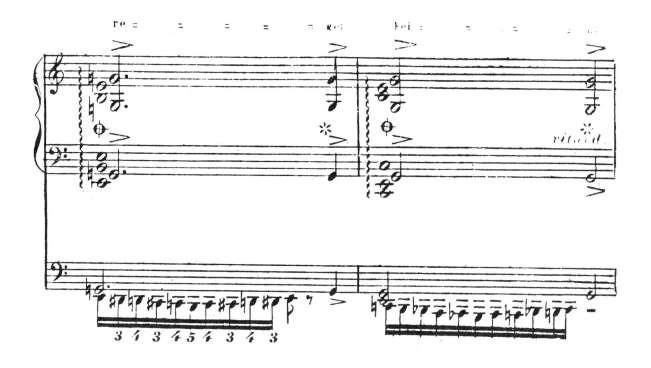

D. et C. Nº 6535.

DIE JUNGE NONNE.

Lied von F. Schubert.

Für das

Piano-Forte

übertragen

von

FR. LISZT.

Eigenthum der Verleger.

Eingetragen in das Vereins-Archiv.

No 6536. WIEN Pr. 1.— C.M.

bei A. Diabelli und Comp.

Graben No 1133.

Die junge Nonne

[THE YOUNG NUN]

Liszt's transcription: R243/6. Transcribed and published 1838.

Schubert's song: D828. Composed 1825. Poem by J. N. Craigher de Jachelutta. Published 1825 as Op. 43, No. 1 (No. 2 is "Nacht und Träume," D827).

Wie braust durch die Wipfel der heulende Sturm!
Es klirren die Balken, es zittert das Haus!
Es rollet der Donner, es leuchtet der Blitz,
Und finster die Nacht, wie das Grab!

Immerhin, immerhin,
   so tobt' es auch jüngst noch in mir!
Es brauste das Leben, wie jetzo der Sturm,
Es bebten die Glieder, wie jetzo das Haus,
Es flammte die Liebe, wie jetzo der Blitz,
Und finster die Brust, wie das Grab.

Nun tobe, du wilder gewalt'ger Sturm,
Im Herzen ist Friede, im Herzen ist Ruh,
Des Bräutigams harret die liebende Braut,
Gereinigt in prüfender Glut,
Der ewigen Liebe getraut.

Ich harre, mein Heiland! mit sehnendem Blick!
Komm, himmlischer Bräutigam, hole die Braut,
Erlöse die Seele von irdischer Haft.

Horch, friedlich ertönet das Glöcklein vom Turm!
Es lockt mich das süße Getön
Allmächtig zu ewigen Höhn.
Alleluja!

How the howling storm roars through the treetops!
The beams groan, the house trembles!
The thunder rolls, the lightning flashes!
And the night is dark as the grave!

Go right on! Go right on!
   That's the way the storm still raged in me too, recently!
Life roared as the storm does now!
My limbs quivered as the house does now!
Love flamed as the lightning does now!
And my heart was dark as the grave!

Now rage, you wild, mighty storm!
In my heart is peace, in my heart is repose!
The loving bride awaits the Bridegroom;
purified in the ordeal of fire,
she is wedded to eternal Love.

I wait, my Savior, with longing gaze!
Come, heavenly Bridegroom, fetch Your bride!
Release my soul from its earthly bondage.

Listen! Peacefully rings the bell from the tower;
the sweet sound lures me
almightily to eternal heights:
hallelujah!

2

DIE JUNGE NONNE.

Lied von Franz Schubert.

Für das Pianoforte übertragen

von

Franz-Liszt.

Ritornello. tremolando sempre legato.

Moderato.

D. et C. Nº 6536.

[61]

braust   durch die Wip =   = fel der heu = len = de Sturm,

es   klir = ren die Bal =   ken, es

zit =   = tert das Haus,

es   rol =   = let der Don =   = ner, es

D. et C. No 6536.

4

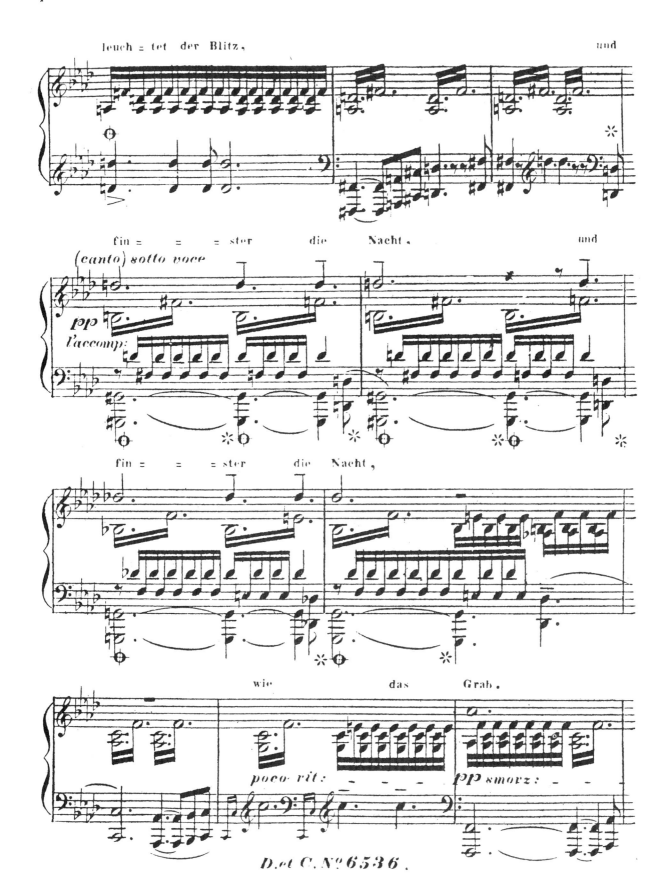

leuch = tet der Blitz,

und

fin = = = ster die Nacht.

und

(canto) sotto voce

pp

l'accomp:

fin = = = ster die Nacht,

wie das Grab.

poco rit:

PP smorz:

D. et C. Nº 6536.

D. et C. Nᵒ 6536.

8

[68]

D.et C. Nº 6536.

12

[71]

D. et C. No 6536.

Frühlingsglaube.

Lied von Fr. Schubert.

für das

Pianoforte

übertragen

von

FR. LISZT.

Eigenthum der Verleger.

Eingetragen in das Vereins-Archiv.

Nº 6537.   **WIEN**   Pr. 30 x C. M.

bei A. Diabelli u. Comp.

Graben Nº 1133.

Frühlingsglaube
[SPRINGTIME FAITH]

Liszt's transcription: R243/7. Transcribed and published 1838.

Schubert's song: D686. Poem by Johann Ludwig Uhland. Two similar versions in B-flat was composed in 1820. A version in A-flat—the basis for Liszt's transcription—was composed in 1822 and published in 1823 as Op. 20, No. 2 (No. 1 is "Sey mir gegrüßt!," D741 [*see p. 2*]; no. 3, "Hänflings Liebeswerbung," D552).

Die linden Lüfte sind erwacht,
Sie säuseln und weben Tag und Nacht,
Sie schaffen an allen Enden.
O frischer Duft, o neuer Klang!
Nun, armes Herze, sei nicht bang!
Nun muß sich alles, alles wenden.

Die Welt wird schöner mit jedem Tag,
Man weiß nicht, was noch werden mag,
Das Blühen will nicht enden.
Es blüht das fernste, tiefste Tal:
Nun, armes Herz, vergiß der Qual!
Nun muß sich alles, alles wenden.

The gentle breezes have awakened,
They murmur and stir day and night,
They are busy in all quarters.
O fresh fragrance, O new sounds!
Now, my poor heart, do not be alarmed!
Now everything, everything must undergo a change.

The world grows more beautiful with each day,
You cannot tell what may still develop,
There is no end to the blossoming.
The farthest, deepest valley is in blossom:
Now, my poor heart, forget your torment!
Now everything, everything must undergo a change.

FRÜHLINGSGLAUBE.

Lied von Franz Schubert.
Für das Pianoforte übertragen
von
Franz Liszt.

Die lin = den Lüf = te
(canto) semplice ma espressivo il canto

sind er = wacht, sie säu = seln und we= = ben

D. et C. Nº 6537.

D.et C.N° 6537.

4

D. et C. No 6537.

Die

Welt wird schö = ner mit je = dem Tag man

weiss nicht, was noch wer = den mag, das

Blü= = = hen will nicht en= = = = den es

D.et C.Nº 6537.

5

[80]

Gretchen am Spinnrade.

Lied von Fr. Schubert.

Für das

PIANO-FORTE

übertragen

von

FR. LISZT.

Eig   der Verleger.
Eingetr   das vereins-Archiv.

Nº 6538.   WIEN   Pr.f 1.— C.M

bei Ant. Diabelli und Comp.

Graben Nº 1133

Gretchen am Spinnrade
[GRETCHEN (MARGARETE) AT THE SPINNING WHEEL]

Liszt's transcription: R243/8. Transcribed and published 1838.

Schubert's song: D118. Text, from *Faust, Part One*, by Johann Wolfgang von Goethe. The composer's first Goethe song, it was published in 1821 as Op. 2.

Meine Ruh ist hin,
Mein Herz ist schwer,

Ich finde sie nimmer
Und nimmermehr.

Wo ich ihn nicht hab
Ist mir das Grab,
Die ganze Welt
Ist mir vergällt.

Mein Armer Kopf
Ist mir verrückt,
Mein armer Sinn
Ist mir zerstückt.

Meine Ruh ist hin,
Mein Herz ist schwer,

Ich finde sie nimmer
Und nimmermehr.

Nach ihm nur schau ich
Zum Fenster hinaus,
Nach ihm nur geh ich
Aus dem Haus.

Sein hoher Gang,
Sein' edle Gestalt,
Seines Mundes Lächeln,
Seiner Augen Gewalt,

Und seiner Rede
Zauberfluß,
Sein Händedruck,
Und ach, sein Kuß!

Meine Ruh ist hin,
Mein Herz ist schwer,
Ich finde sie nimmer
Und nimmermehr.

Mein Busen drängt
Sich nach ihm hin.
Ach dürft ich fassen
Und halten ihn,

Und küssen ihn,
So wie ich wollt,
An seinen Küssen
Vergehen sollt!

[Meine Ruh ist hin,
Mein Herz
        ist schwer . . .]

My heart is heavy,
my peace of mind
    is gone;
I'll never get it back,
never get it back.

Any place without him
is the grave to me;
the whole world
is soured for me;

my poor head
is crazed,
my poor mind
is shattered.

My heart is heavy,
my peace of mind
    is gone;
I'll never get it back,
never get it back.

If I look out the window,
it's only for him;
if I go outdoors,
it's only in hopes
    of seeing him.

His fine gait,
his noble figure,
the smile on his lips,
the power in his eyes,

and the magical flow
of his speech,
the pressure of his hands,
and oh, his kiss!

My heart is heavy,
my peace of mind is gone;
I'll never get it back,
never get it back.

My heart yearns
for him;
oh, if I could embrace him
and hold him,

and kiss him
as I would like to;
if I could die
kissing him!

[My heart is heavy,
my peace of mind
    is gone . . .]

GRETCHEN AM SPINNRADE.

Lied von Franz Schubert.

Für das Pianoforte übertragen

von

Franz Liszt.

Pas trop vite
Nicht zu geschwind

Meine un poco

marcato il canto

Ruh _____ ist hin _____, mein Herz _____ ist

schwer. ich fin = = de, ich fin = = = de sie

nim = = mer und nim = = = = mer = mehr!

D. et C. Nº 6538.

[85]

D. et C. N.º 6538.

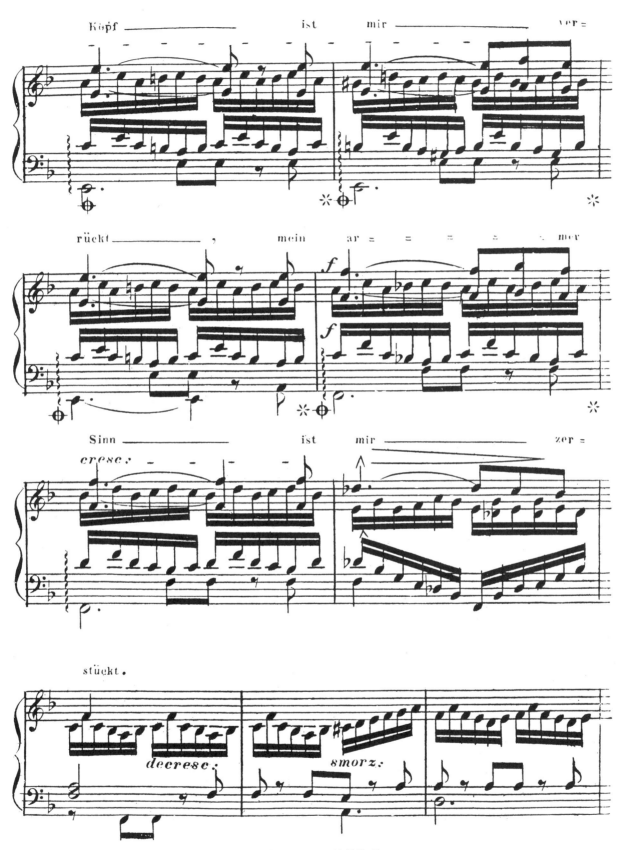

D.et C.Nº 6538.

8

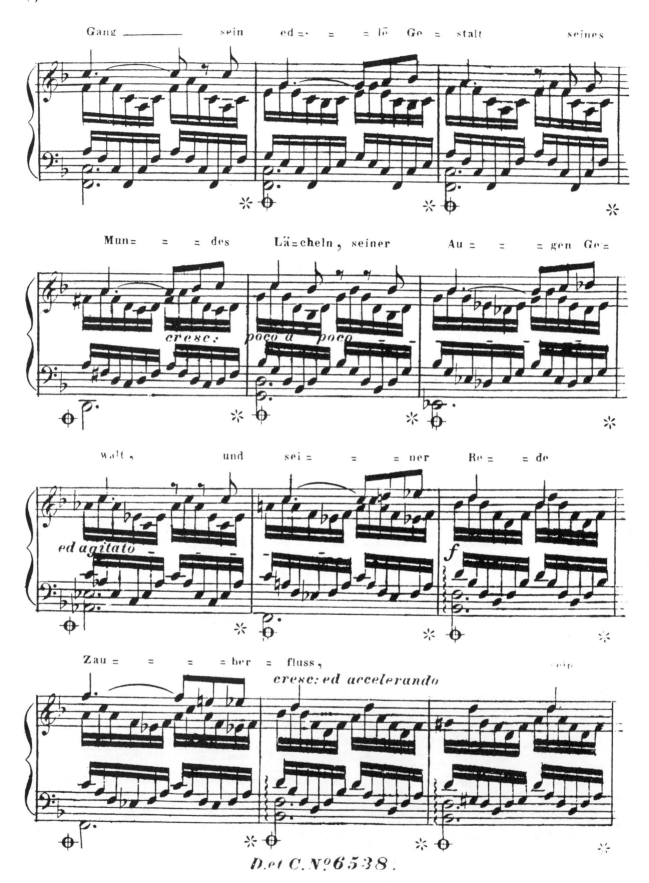

10

D.et C.Nº 6538.

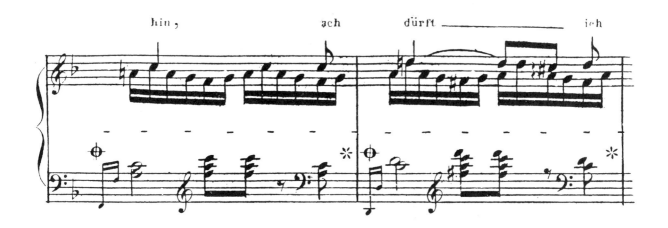

D. et C. Nᵒ 6538 .

12

D.et C.Nº 6538.

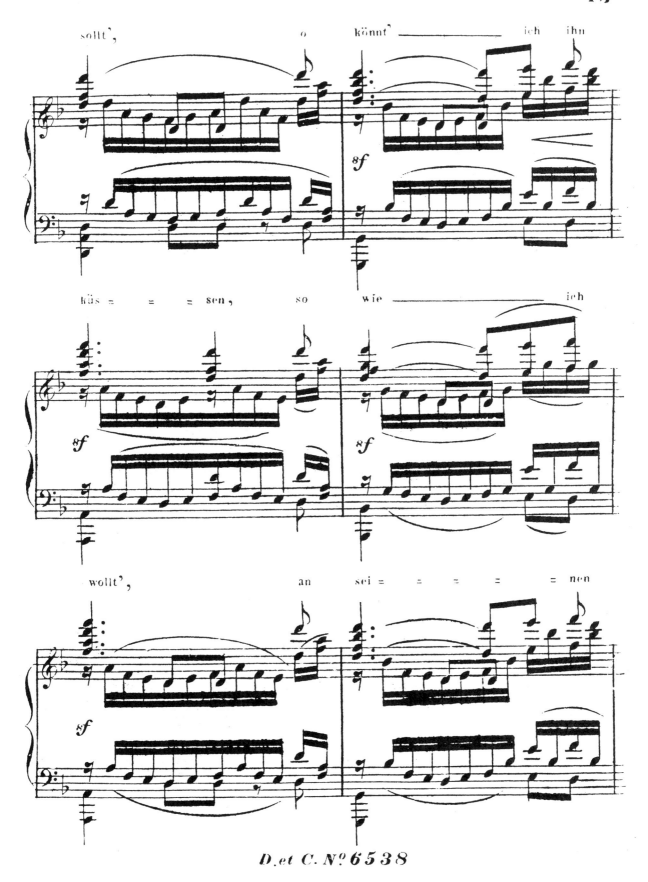

D. et C. Nº 6538

14

D.et C.N° 6538.

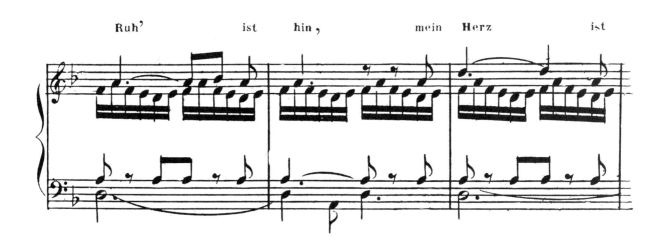

D.et C.N° 6538.

9

Ständchen von Shakespeare.

LIED

von

FR. SCHUBERT.

Für das

Piano Forte

übertragen von

Fr. Liszt.

Eigenthum der Verleger
Eingetragen in das Vereins-Archiv.

№ 6539.   WIEN   Pr._45 x C.M.

bei Ant. Diabelli u. Comp.

Graben № 1133.

Ständchen von Shakespeare
[SERENADE BY SHAKESPEARE]

Liszt's transcription: R243/9. Transcribed and published 1838.

Schubert's song: D889. Composed 1826. Published 1830. The poem—"Hark, hark! the lark!" from Act II, Scene III of Shakespeare's play *Cymbeline*—was translated from English to German by August Wilhelm von Schlegel. The second and third stanzas in the first edition of the song setting were translated by Friedrich Reil.

Schubert's other, better known, "Ständchen" ["Leise flehen meine Lieder"], a setting of a poem by Ludwig Rellstab, is the fourth of his *Schwanengesang* settings, D957/4, composed 1828, published 1829.

Horch, horch! die Lerch' im Ätherblau;
und Phöbus, neuerweckt,
tränkt seine Rosse mit dem Thau,
der Blumenkelche deckt;

der Ringelblume Knospe schleußt
die goldnen Äuglein auf;
mit allem, was da reizend heißt,
du süße Maid steh auf!

Hark, hark! the lark at heaven's gate sings,
And Phœbus 'gins arise,
His steeds to water at those springs
On chaliced flowers that lies;

And winking Mary-buds begin
To ope their golden eyes;
With every thing that pretty is,
My lady sweet, arise:
Arise, arise!

STÄNDCHEN von SHAKESPEARE.

Lied von Franz Schubert.
Für das Pianoforte übertragen
von
Franz Liszt.

Allegretto.

Horch, horch, die Lerch' im Äther = blau, und

D. et C. No 6539.

D. et C. N.º 6539.

auf, steh auf, du süs=se Maid steh auf!

Wenn schon die lie = = be gan = = ze Nacht, der

Ster = = ne lich = = tes Heer hoch

ü = = ber dir im Wech = = sel wacht, so

D. et C. N? 6539.

8

D.et C. N.º 6539.

[105]

D. et C. N° 8539.

16

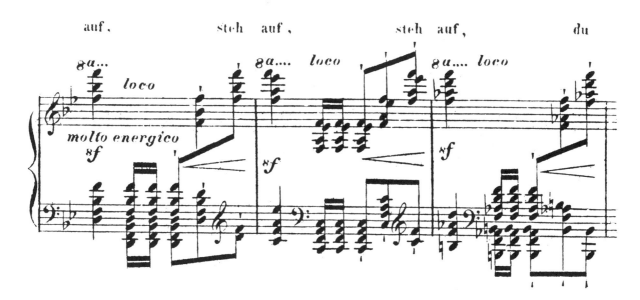

D. et C. Nº 6539.

[107]

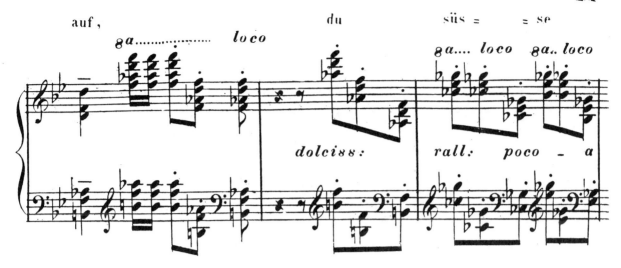

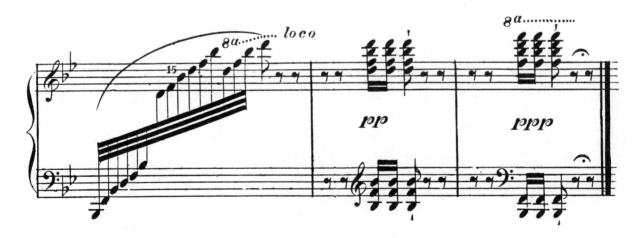

11

D. et C. Nº 6539.

Rastlose Liebe.

Lied von Fr. Schubert.

Für das

PIANO-FORTE

übertragen

von

FR. LISZT.

Nº 6540.

Eigenthum der Verleger.
Eingetragen in das Vereins-Archiv.

Pr. 30 x C.M.

WIEN

bei Ant. Diabelli und Comp.

Graben Nº 1133.

Rastlose Liebe

[RESTLESS LOVE]

Liszt's transcription: R243/10. Transcribed and published 1838.

Schubert's song: D138. Composed 1815. Poem by Johann Wolfgang von Goethe. Published 1821 as the first of five Goethe settings, Op. 5 (No. 2 is "Nähe des Geliebten," D162; No. 3, "Der Fischer," D225; No. 4, "Erster Verlust," D226; No. 5, "Der König in Thule" (from *Faust*), D367.

Dem Schnee, dem Regen,	Into the snow, the rain,
Dem Wind entgegen,	The wind,
Im Dampf der Klüfte,	In the vapor of the chasms,
Durch Nebeldüfte,	Through misty haze,
Immer zu! Immer zu!	Onward! Onward!
Ohne Rast und Ruh!	Without rest or repose!
Lieber durch Leiden	I would rather force my way
Möcht ich mich schlagen,	Through sorrows
Als so viel Freuden	Than to endure so many
Des Lebens ertragen.	Joys of life.
Alle das Neigen	All the inclination
Von Herzen zu Herzen,	Of one heart to another,
Ach, wie so eigen	Oh, how oddly
Schaffet das Schmerzen!	It causes pain!
Wie Soll ich fliehen?	How shall I flee?
Wälderwärts ziehen?	Journey toward the woods?
Alles vergebens!	All in vain!
Krone des Lebens,	The crown of life,
Glück ohne Ruh,	Happiness without repose:
Liebe, bist du!	Love, that is what you are!

RASTLOSE LIEBE.

Lied von Franz Schubert.

Für das Pianoforte übertragen

von

Franz Liszt.

Presto molto appassionato.

D. et C. No 6540.

im = = = mer zu, im = = mer zu,

ff precipitato

oh = = = ne Rast und

ga..... loco

rf

dim: subito

Ruh ! Lie = ber durch Lei = den

ga............ loco

p leggero

dol: sempre agitato ed appassio =

wollt' ich mich schla = = gen, als so

nato cresc: _

Det C. Nº 6540.

Wie soll ich flih'n? Wäl = =der = wärt

con smania

zieh'n? al = = =les, al = = =

=les ver = ge = bens!

loco

p più dim:

D. et C. N⁰ 6540.

D.et C.Nº 6540.

DER WANDERER.

Lied von Fr. Schubert.

Für das

PIANO-FORTE

übertragen von

FR. LISZT.

Eigenthum der Verleger.

Eingetragen in das Vereins-Archiv.

No 6541. WIEN Pr. 45 x C.M.

bei Ant. Diabelli und Comp.

Graben No 1133.

Der Wanderer

[THE WANDERER]

Liszt's transcription: R243/11. Transcribed and published 1838.

Schubert's song: D493/489. Composed after October 1816. The poem by G. P. Schmidt von Lübeck, originally entitled "Des Fremdlings Abendlied" ["The Stranger's Evening Song], was published as "Der Unglückliche" ["The Unhappy Man"] and first set by Schubert under that title, along with its misattribution to "Z. Werner." A revised setting entitled "Der Wanderer"—the basis for Liszt's transcription—was published in 1821 as Op. 4, No. 1 (No. 2 is "Morgenlied," D685; No. 3, "Wandrers Nachtlied," D224).

Schubert's *Wandererfantasie* (Fantasy in C), a four-movement work for solo piano, Op. 15 (D760, 1822), uses the song as the basis for its second movement (Adagio). Liszt's arrangement of the complete work for piano and orchestra followed in 1851.

Ich komme vom Gebirge her,
Es dampft das Tal, es braust das Meer.
Ich wandle still, bin wenig froh,
Und immer fragt der Seufzer, wo?

I arrive from the mountains;
the valley is steamy with mist, the sea roars.
I walk in silence, am seldom happy,
and my sighs always ask "Where?"

Die Sonne dünkt mich hier so kalt,
Die Blüte welk, das Leben alt,
Und was sie reden leerer Schall;
Ich bin ein Fremdling überall.

The sun here seems so cold to me,
the blossoms seem withered, life seems old,
and what people say seems empty noise—
I am a stranger everywhere.

Wo bist du, mein geliebtes Land?
Gesucht, geahnt, und nie gekannt!

Where are you, country that I love?
I seek for you, I have premonitions of you,
   but I never know you!

Das Land, das Land so hoffnungsgrün,
Das Land, wo meine Rosen blühn.

That land, that land so green with hope,
that land where my roses bloom,

Wo meine Freunde wandelnd gehn,
Wo meine Toten auferstehn,
Das Land, das meine Sprache spricht,
O Land, wo bist du? . . .

where my friends walk up and down,
where my departed ones come back to life,
the land that speaks my language—
O land, where are you?

Ich wandle still, bin wenig froh,
Und immer fragt der Seufzer, wo?
Im Geisterhauch tönt's mir zurück:
'Dort, wo du nicht bist, dort ist das Glück.'

I walk in silence, am seldom happy,
and my sighs always ask "Where?"
In a ghostly breath, the echo replies to me:
"Where you are not, there happiness is."

DER WANDERER.

Lied von Franz Schubert.

Für das Pianoforte übertragen

von

Franz Liszt.

Lento assai.

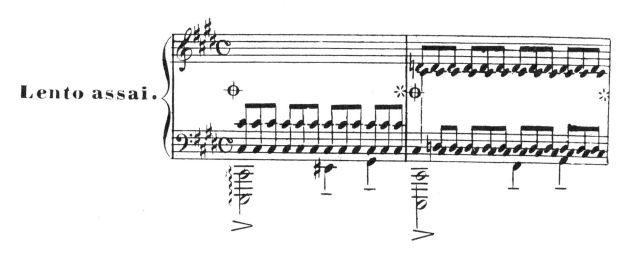

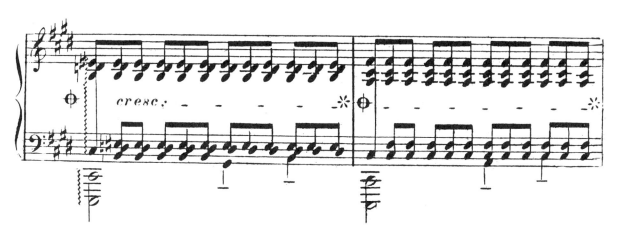

D. et C. N.º 6541.

Jch komme vom Gebirge

Meer.

Ich wan = dle still, bin we = = nig

D. et C. N° 3541.

bist du, wo bist du, mein gelieb = tes

Più animato.

con anima

delicatamente

Land? ge = sucht_____, ge = altnt_____,

string:

und nie ge =

ritard:

kannt. Das Land, das Land so hoffnungsgrün, so

Allegro vivo.

ga........................loco

dol:

f

D. et C. No 6541.

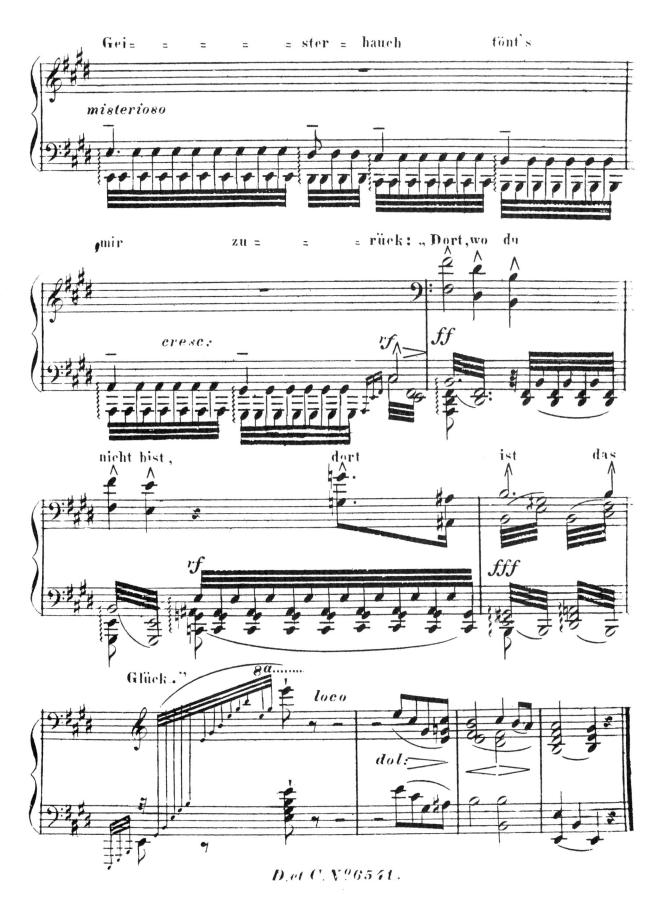

AVE MARIA.

Lied von Fr. Schubert.

Für das

Pianoforte

übertragen

von

FR. LISZT.

Eigenthum der Verleger.

Eingetragen in das Vereins Archiv.

Nº 6542.

Pr. f 1.— C.M.

WIEN,

bei Ant. Diabelli und Comp.

Graben Nº 1133.

Ave Maria
(Hymne an die Jungfrau)
[HYMN TO THE VIRGIN]

Liszt's transcription: R243/12. Transcribed and published 1838.

Schubert's song: D839. Composed 1825. One of seven settings of texts from Sir Walter Scott's poem "The Lady of the Lake," translated from English to German by Adam Storck. The complete set was published in 1826 as Op. 52, Nos. 1–7. The sixth song of the set, "Ellens Gesang III" ["Ellen's Song III"], is a setting of a nonliturgical text beginning with the words "Ave Maria."

Ave Maria! Jungfrau mild!
  Erhöre einer Jungfrau Flehen!
Aus diesem Felsen, starr und wild,
  soll mein Gebet zu dir hinwehen.
Wir schlafen sicher bis zum Morgen,
  ob Menschen noch so grausam sind.
O Jungfrau, sieh' der Jungfrau Sorgen,
  o Mutter, hör' ein bittend Kind!
                    Ave Maria!

Ave Maria! maiden mild!
  Listen to a maiden's prayer!
Thou canst hear though from the wild,
  Thou canst save amid despair.
Safe may we sleep beneath thy care,
  Though banish'd, outcast, and reviled;
Maiden! hear a maiden's prayer-
  Mother, hear a suppliant child!
                    Ave Maria!

Ave Maria! Unbefleckt!
  Wenn wir auf diesen Fels hinsinken
zum Schlaf, und uns dein Schutz bedeckt,
  wird weich der harte Fels uns dünken.
Du lächelst, Rosendüfte wehen
  in dieser dumpfen Felsengruft.
O Mutter, höre Kindes Flehen,
  o Jungfrau, eine Jungfrau ruft!
                    Ave Maria!

Ave Maria! undefiled!
  The flinty couch we now must share
Shall seem with down of eider piled,
  If thy protection hover there.
The murky cavern's heavy air
  Shall breathe of balm if thou hast smiled;
Then, Maiden! hear a maiden's prayer;
  Mother, list a suppliant child!
                    Ave Maria!

Ave Maria! Reine Magd!
  Der Erde und der Luft Dämonen,
von deines Auges Huld verjagt,
  sie können hier nicht bei uns wohnen!
Wir woll'n uns still dem Schicksal beugen,
  da uns dein heil'ger Trost anweht;
der Jungfrau wolle hold dich neigen,
  dem Kind, das für den Vater fleht!
                    Ave Maria!

Ave Maria! stainless styled!
  Foul demons of the earth and air,
From this their wonted haunt exiled,
  Shall flee before thy presence fair.
We bow us to our lot of care,
  Beneath thy guidance reconciled;
Hear for a maid a maiden's prayer,
  And for a father hear a child!
                    Ave Maria!

AVE MARIA.

Lied von Franz Schubert.

Für das Pianoforte übertragen

von

Franz Liszt.

(*) Les notes tournées en haut, doivent être exécutées par la main droite, celles tournées en bas par la main gauche.

D. et C. N.º 6542.

wild,   soll mein Gebeth zu dir hin=

we = = = = = hen.   Wir

smorz:

il canto

schla = = fen si = cher bis zum Mor = gen,   ob

sempre ben marcato

D. et C. N.º 6542.

cresc: _ _ _ _ _ _ _ _

Men = = schen, noch so grausam sind .   O

string: _ _ _ _ _ rf

Jung = = frau , sieh der Jungfrau Sor = gen ,   o

rf

D. et C. No 6542.

[134]

radolcendo　　　　　　　　　　　　　　　*smorz:*

Mut = = ter hör' ein bittend Kind!

poco riten: — — — — —

dolciss:

A = = = ve Ma = ri = = = = =

sotto voce

dolciss:

D. et C. No 6542.

10

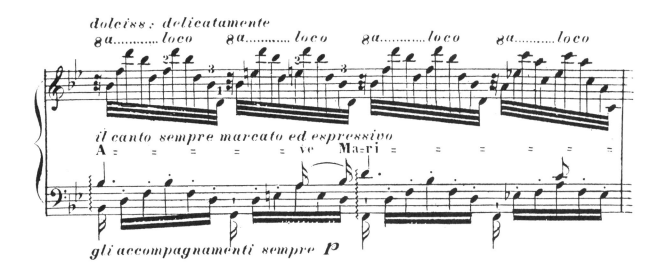

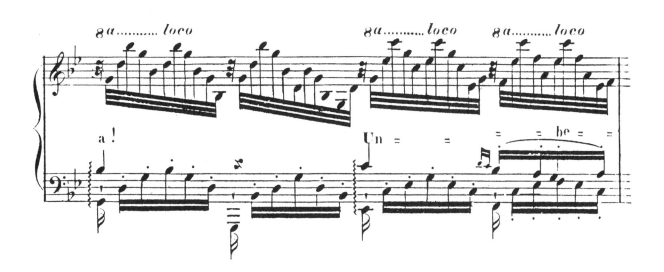

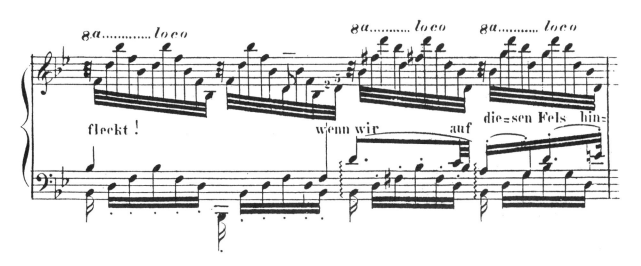

D. et C. N.º 6542.

[137]

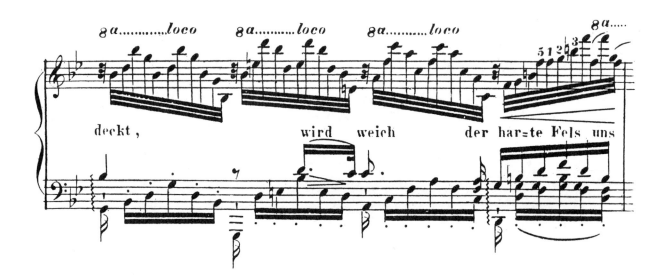

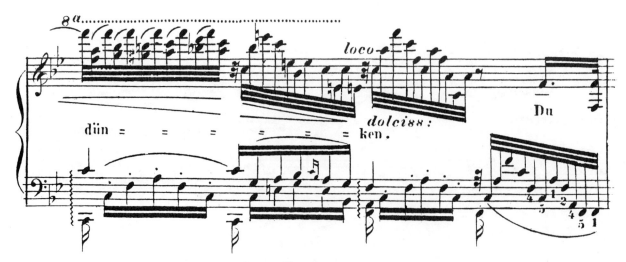

D.et C.Nº6542.

12

D. et C. Nº 6542.

D. et C. N.° 6542.

D. et C. Nº 6542.

END OF EDITION

Dover Piano and Keyboard Editions

Albeniz, Isaac, IBERIA AND ESPAÑA: Two Complete Works for Solo Piano. Spanish composer's greatest piano works in authoritative editions. Includes the popular "Tango." 192pp. 9 x 12. 25367-8

Bach, Carl Philipp Emanuel, GREAT KEYBOARD SONATAS. Comprehensive two-volume edition contains 51 sonatas by second, most prestigious son of Johann Sebastian Bach. Originality, rich harmony, delicate workmanship. Authoritative French edition. Total of 384pp. 8⅜ x 11¼.
Series I 24853-4
Series II 24854-2

Bach, Johann Sebastian, COMPLETE KEYBOARD TRANSCRIPTIONS OF CONCERTOS BY BAROQUE COMPOSERS. Sixteen concertos by Vivaldi, Telemann and others, transcribed for solo keyboard instruments. Bach-Gesellschaft edition. 128pp. 9⅜ x 12¼. 25529-8

Bach, Johann Sebastian, COMPLETE PRELUDES AND FUGUES FOR ORGAN. All 25 of Bach's complete sets of preludes and fugues (i.e. compositions written as pairs), from the authoritative Bach-Gesellschaft edition. 168pp. 8⅜ x 11. 24816-X

Bach, Johann Sebastian, ITALIAN CONCERTO, CHROMATIC FANTASIA AND FUGUE AND OTHER WORKS FOR KEYBOARD. Sixteen of Bach's best-known, most-performed and most-recorded works for the keyboard, reproduced from the authoritative Bach-Gesellschaft edition. 112pp. 9 x 12. 25387-2

Bach, Johann Sebastian, KEYBOARD MUSIC. Bach-Gesellschaft edition. For harpsichord, piano, other keyboard instruments. English Suites, French Suites, Six Partitas, Goldberg Variations, Two-Part Inventions, Three-Part Sinfonias. 312pp. 8⅛ x 11. 22360-4

Bach, Johann Sebastian, ORGAN MUSIC. Bach-Gesellschaft edition. 93 works. 6 Trio Sonatas, German Organ Mass, Orgelbüchlein, Six Schubler Chorales, 18 Choral Preludes. 357pp. 8⅛ x 11. 22359-0

Bach, Johann Sebastian, TOCCATAS, FANTASIAS, PASSACAGLIA AND OTHER WORKS FOR ORGAN. Over 20 best-loved works including Toccata and Fugue in D Minor, BWV 565; Passacaglia and Fugue in C Minor, BWV 582, many more. Bach-Gesellschaft edition. 176pp. 9 x 12. 25403-8

Bach, Johann Sebastian, TWO- AND THREE-PART INVENTIONS. Reproduction of original autograph ms. Edited by Eric Simon. 62pp. 8⅛ x 11. 21982-8

Bach, Johann Sebastian, THE WELL-TEMPERED CLAVIER: Books I and II, Complete. All 48 preludes and fugues in all major and minor keys. Authoritative Bach-Gesellschaft edition. Explanation of ornaments in English, tempo indications, music corrections. 208pp. 9⅜ x 12¼. 24532-2

Bartók, Béla, PIANO MUSIC OF BÉLA BARTÓK, Series I. New, definitive Archive Edition incorporating composer's corrections. Includes *Funeral March* from *Kossuth, Fourteen Bagatelles,* Bartók's break to modernism. 167pp. 9 x 12. (Available in U.S. only) 24108-4

Bartók, Béla, PIANO MUSIC OF BÉLA BARTÓK, Series II. Second in the Archive Edition incorporating composer's corrections. 85 short pieces *For Children, Two Elegies, Two Romanian Dances,* etc. 192pp. 9 x 12. (Available in U.S. only) 24109-2

Beethoven, Ludwig van, BAGATELLES, RONDOS AND OTHER SHORTER WORKS FOR PIANO. Most popular and most performed shorter works, including Rondo a capriccio in G and Andante in F. Breitkopf & Härtel edition. 128pp. 9⅜ x 12¼. 25392-9

Beethoven, Ludwig van, COMPLETE PIANO SONATAS. All sonatas in fine Schenker edition, with fingering, analytical material. One of best modern editions. 615pp. 9 x 12. Two-vol. set. 23134-8, 23135-6

Beethoven, Ludwig van, COMPLETE VARIATIONS FOR SOLO PIANO, Ludwig van Beethoven. Contains all 21 sets of Beethoven's piano variations, including the extremely popular *Diabelli Variations, Op. 120.* 240pp. 9⅜ x 12¼. 25188-8

Blesh, Rudi (ed.), CLASSIC PIANO RAGS. Best ragtime music (1897–1922) by Scott Joplin, James Scott, Joseph F. Lamb, Tom Turpin, nine others. 364pp. 9 x 12. Introduction by Blesh. 20469-3

Brahms, Johannes, COMPLETE SHORTER WORKS FOR SOLO PIANO. All solo music not in other two volumes. Waltzes, Scherzo in E Flat Minor, Eight Pieces, Rhapsodies, Fantasies, Intermezzi, etc. Vienna Gesellschaft der Musikfreunde. 180pp. 9 x 12. 22651-4

Brahms, Johannes, COMPLETE SONATAS AND VARIATIONS FOR SOLO PIANO. All sonatas, five variations on themes from Schumann, Paganini, Handel, etc. Vienna Gesellschaft der Musikfreunde edition. 178pp. 9 x 12. 22650-6

Brahms, Johannes, COMPLETE TRANSCRIPTIONS, CADENZAS AND EXERCISES FOR SOLO PIANO. Vienna Gesellschaft der Musikfreunde edition, vol. 15. Studies after Chopin, Weber, Bach; gigues, sarabandes; 10 Hungarian dances, etc. 178pp. 9 x 12. 22652-2

Buxtehude, Dietrich, ORGAN WORKS. Complete organ works of extremely influential pre-Bach composer. Toccatas, preludes, chorales, more. Definitive Breitkopf & Härtel edition. 320pp. 8⅜ x 11¼. (Available in U.S. only) 25682-0

Byrd, William, MY LADY NEVELLS BOOKE OF VIRGINAL MUSIC. 42 compositions in modern notation from 1591 ms. For any keyboard instrument. 245pp. 8⅛ x 11. 22246-2

Chopin, Frédéric, COMPLETE BALLADES, IMPROMPTUS AND SONATAS. The four Ballades, four Impromptus and three Sonatas. Authoritative Mikuli edition. 192pp. 9 x 12. 24164-5

Chopin, Frédéric, COMPLETE MAZURKAS, Frédéric Chopin. 51 best-loved compositions, reproduced directly from the authoritative Kistner edition edited by Carl Mikuli. 160pp. 9 x 12. 25548-4

Chopin, Frédéric, COMPLETE PRELUDES AND ETUDES FOR SOLO PIANO. All 25 Preludes and all 27 Etudes by greatest piano music composer. Authoritative Mikuli edition. 192pp. 9 x 12. 24052-5

Chopin, Frédéric, FANTASY IN F MINOR, BARCAROLLE, BERCEUSE AND OTHER WORKS FOR SOLO PIANO. 15 works, including one of the greatest of the Romantic period, the Fantasy in F Minor, Op. 49, reprinted from the authoritative German edition prepared by Chopin's student, Carl Mikuli. 224pp. 8⅜ x 11¼. 25950-1

Chopin, Frédéric, NOCTURNES AND POLONAISES. 20 *Nocturnes* and 11 *Polonaises* reproduced from the authoritative Mikuli edition for pianists, students, and musicologists. Commentary. 224pp. 9 x 12. 24564-0

Chopin, Frédéric, WALTZES AND SCHERZOS. All of the Scherzos and nearly all (20) of the Waltzes from the authoritative Mikuli edition. Editorial commentary. 160pp. 9 x 12. 24316-8

Cofone, Charles J. F. (ed.), ELIZABETH ROGERS HIR VIRGINALL BOOKE. All 112 pieces from noted 1656 manuscript, most never before published. Composers include Thomas Brewer, William Byrd, Orlando Gibbons, etc. Calligraphy by editor. 125pp. 9 x 12. 23138-0

Dover Piano and Keyboard Editions

Couperin, François, KEYBOARD WORKS/Series One: Ordres I–XIII; Series Two: Ordres XIV–XXVII and Miscellaneous Pieces. Over 200 pieces. Reproduced directly from edition prepared by Johannes Brahms and Friedrich Chrysander. Total of 496pp. 8⅝ x 11.
Series I 25795-9
Series II 25796-7

Debussy, Claude, COMPLETE PRELUDES, Books 1 and 2. 24 evocative works that reveal the essence of Debussy's genius for musical imagery, among them many of the composer's most famous piano compositions. Glossary of French terms. 128pp. 8⅜ x 11¼. 25970-6

Debussy, Claude, DEBUSSY MASTERPIECES FOR SOLO PIANO: 20 Works. From France's most innovative and influential composer–a rich compilation of works that include "Golliwogg's cakewalk," "Engulfed cathedral," "Clair de lune," and 17 others. 128pp. 9 x 12. 42425-1

Debussy, Claude, PIANO MUSIC 1888–1905. Deux Arabesques, Suite Bergamesque, Masques, first series of Images, etc. Nine others, in corrected editions. 175pp. 9⅜ x 12¼. 22771-5

Dvořák, Antonín, HUMORESQUES AND OTHER WORKS FOR SOLO PIANO. Humoresques, Op. 101, complete, Silhouettes, Op. 8, Poetic Tone Pictures, Theme with Variations, Op. 36, 4 Slavonic Dances, more. 160pp. 9 x 12. 28355-0

Fauré, Gabriel, COMPLETE PRELUDES, IMPROMPTUS AND VALSES-CAPRICES. Eighteen elegantly wrought piano works in authoritative editions. Only one-volume collection available. 144pp. 9 x 12. (Not available in France or Germany) 25789-4

Fauré, Gabriel, NOCTURNES AND BARCAROLLES FOR SOLO PIANO. 12 nocturnes and 12 barcarolles reprinted from authoritative French editions. 208pp. 9⅜ x 12¼. (Not available in France or Germany) 27955-3

Feofanov, Dmitry (ed.), RARE MASTERPIECES OF RUSSIAN PIANO MUSIC: Eleven Pieces by Glinka, Balakirev, Glazunov and Others. Glinka's *Prayer,* Balakirev's *Reverie,* Liapunov's *Transcendental Etude, Op. 11, No. 10,* and eight others–full, authoritative scores from Russian texts. 144pp. 9 x 12. 24659-0

Franck, César, ORGAN WORKS. Composer's best-known works for organ, including Six Pieces, Trois Pieces, and Trois Chorals. Oblong format for easy use at keyboard. Authoritative Durand edition. 208pp. 11⅜ x 8¼. 25517-4

Franck, César, SELECTED PIANO COMPOSITIONS, edited by Vincent d'Indy. Outstanding selection of influential French composer's piano works, including early pieces and the two masterpieces–Prelude, Choral and Fugue; and Prelude, Aria and Finale. Ten works in all. 138pp. 9 x 12. 23269-7

Gillespie, John (ed.), NINETEENTH-CENTURY EUROPEAN PIANO MUSIC: Unfamiliar Masterworks. Difficult-to-find etudes, toccatas, polkas, impromptus, waltzes, etc., by Albéniz, Bizet, Chabrier, Fauré, Smetana, Richard Strauss, Wagner and 16 other composers. 62 pieces. 343pp. 9 x 12. (Not available in France or Germany) 23447-9

Gottschalk, Louis M., PIANO MUSIC. 26 pieces (including covers) by early 19th-century American genius. "Bamboula," "The Banjo," other Creole, Negro-based material, through elegant salon music. 301pp. 9¼ x 12. 21683-7

Granados, Enrique, GOYESCAS, SPANISH DANCES AND OTHER WORKS FOR SOLO PIANO. Great Spanish composer's most admired, most performed suites for the piano, in definitive Spanish editions. 176pp. 9 x 12. 25481-X

Grieg, Edvard, COMPLETE LYRIC PIECES FOR PIANO. All 66 pieces from Grieg's ten sets of little mood pictures for piano, favorites of generations of pianists. 224pp. 9⅜ x 12¼. 26176-X

Handel, G. F., KEYBOARD WORKS FOR SOLO INSTRUMENTS. 35 neglected works from Handel's vast oeuvre, originally jotted down as improvisations. Includes Eight Great Suites, others. New sequence. 174pp. 9⅜ x 12¼. 24338-9

Haydn, Joseph, COMPLETE PIANO SONATAS. 52 sonatas reprinted from authoritative Breitkopf & Härtel edition. Extremely clear and readable; ample space for notes, analysis. 464pp. 9⅜ x 12¼. Vol. I 24726-0
Vol. II 24727-9

Jasen, David A. (ed.), RAGTIME GEMS: Original Sheet Music for 25 Ragtime Classics. Includes original sheet music and covers for 25 rags, including three of Scott Joplin's finest: "Searchlight Rag," "Rose Leaf Rag," and "Fig Leaf Rag." 122pp. 9 x 12. 25248-5

Joplin, Scott, COMPLETE PIANO RAGS. All 38 piano rags by the acknowledged master of the form, reprinted from the publisher's original editions complete with sheet music covers. Introduction by David A. Jasen. 208pp. 9 x 12. 25807-6

Liszt, Franz, ANNÉES DE PÈLERINAGE, COMPLETE. Authoritative Russian edition of piano masterpieces: *Première Année (Suisse): Deuxième Année (Italie)* and *Venezia e Napoli; Troisième Année,* other related pieces. 288pp. 9⅜ x 12¼. 25627-8

Liszt, Franz, BEETHOVEN SYMPHONIES NOS. 6–9 TRANSCRIBED FOR SOLO PIANO. Includes Symphony No. 6 in F major, Op. 68, "Pastorale"; Symphony No. 7 in A major, Op. 92; Symphony No. 8 in F major, Op. 93; and Symphony No. 9 in D minor, Op. 125, "Choral." A memorable tribute from one musical genius to another. 224pp. 9 x 12. 41884-7

Liszt, Franz, COMPLETE ETUDES FOR SOLO PIANO, Series I: Including the Transcendental Etudes, edited by Busoni. Also includes Etude in 12 Exercises, 12 Grandes Etudes and Mazeppa. Breitkopf & Härtel edition. 272pp. 8⅝ x 11¼. 25815-7

Liszt, Franz, COMPLETE ETUDES FOR SOLO PIANO, Series II: Including the Paganini Etudes and Concert Etudes, edited by Busoni. Also includes Morceau de Salon, Ab Irato. Breitkopf & Härtel edition. 192pp. 8⅝ x 11¼. 25816-5

Liszt, Franz, COMPLETE HUNGARIAN RHAPSODIES FOR SOLO PIANO. All 19 Rhapsodies reproduced directly from authoritative Russian edition. All headings, footnotes translated to English. 224pp. 8⅝ x 11¼. 24744-9

Liszt, Franz, MEPHISTO WALTZ AND OTHER WORKS FOR SOLO PIANO. Rapsodie Espagnole, Liebestraüme Nos. 1–3, Valse Oubliée No. 1, Nuages Gris, Polonaises Nos. 1 and 2, Grand Galop Chromatique, more. 192pp. 8⅝ x 11¼. 28147-7

Liszt, Franz, PIANO TRANSCRIPTIONS FROM FRENCH AND ITALIAN OPERAS. Virtuoso transformations of themes by Mozart, Verdi, Bellini, other masters, into unforgettable music for piano. Published in association with American Liszt Society. 247pp. 9 x 12. 24273-0

Liszt, Franz, SONATA IN B MINOR AND OTHER WORKS FOR PIANO. One of Liszt's most frequently performed piano masterpieces, with the six Consolations, ten *Harmonies poetiques et religieuses,* two Ballades and two Legendes. Breitkopf & Härtel edition. 208pp. 8⅝ x 11¼. 26182-4

Maitland, J. Fuller, Squire, W. B. (eds.), THE FITZWILLIAM VIRGINAL BOOK. Famous early 17th-century collection of keyboard music, 300 works by Morley, Byrd, Bull, Gibbons, etc. Modern notation. Total of 938pp. 8⅞ x 11. Two-vol. set. 21068-5, 21069-3

Available from your music dealer or write for ***free*** *Music Catalog to*
Dover Publications, Inc., Dept. MUBI, 31 East 2nd Street, Mineola, NY 11501
Visit us online at ***www.doverpublications.com***